THE FACE OF A MAN

ethan HUBBARD

THE FACE OF A MAN

images

from around the world

The Pilgrim Press

Cleveland, Ohio

The Pilgrim Press, Cleveland, Ohio 44115

Printed in the United States of America on acid-free paper

02 01 00 99 98 97   5 4 3 2 1

Library of Congress Cataloging-in-Publication Data

Hubbard, Ethan, 1941 –

    The face of a man : images from around the world / Ethan Hubbard.

       p.   cm.

    ISBN 0-8298-1168-0 (cloth : alk. paper)

     1. Men—Cross-cultural studies. 2. Men—Portraits.

   I. Title.

HQ1090.H83   1997

305.31'022'2–DC21

96-49749

CIP

r97

May all beings enjoy happiness

and the sources of happiness.

May all be free from sorrow

and the sources of sorrow.

May all never be separated from the sacred happiness

which is sorrowless.

And may all live in equanimity,

without too much attachment and too much aversion,

and live believing in the equality of all that lives.

In the spring of 1978, nearing my thirty-seventh year and determined to bring a deeper sense of fulfillment into my life, I sold my house and land in northern Vermont and began spending as much time as possible with rural and indigenous people.

For the previous ten years I had worked as the deputy director of the Vermont Historical Society, collecting and preserving artifacts for the Vermont Museum and Library. Whenever I felt overwhelmed by my desk work, I checked out of the office with a couple of cameras and a tape recorder and would visit interesting Vermonters: loggers, farmers, homesteaders, and especially the elders whose life stories brought me no end of pleasure and inspiration. I realized that interviewing and photographing people was the work that I wanted to do with my life. In 1978 I left Vermont and began to travel.

My first real adventure was a two-year ramble around the United States in an old VW camper, complete with cameras and my dog Willow. Between 1978 and 1980 I drove the back roads of rural America, stopping to visit with interesting people who were leading lives very different from mine. The Native Americans especially interested me—the Navajos, Apaches, Sioux, and the Tohono O'odham. I traveled to their lands in my VW bus with camping gear stashed beneath the bed. I always managed to find elders who seemed happy to have me about. I would sit at their feet and ask questions from my heart, and the visits flowed from minutes into days.

It was an America I had forgotten existed—a land of wide open spaces to set my mind free, a land of tiny prairie villages with welcoming cafes, church socials, and friendly people enjoying good talk on the streets. I shared coffee with cowboys in Wyoming, danced with Cajuns after the rice harvest in Louisiana, herded cattle with Idaho schoolchildren, and brought in winter wood with Southerners and their mules. Each gentle man seemed to show me the next piece to my puzzle. Where mainstream America had often misled me, my travels reacquainted me with my true self. I felt righted like a listing ship in a troubled sea.

In 1980 I began traveling farther afield: the Outer Hebrides of Scotland, Mexico's Sierra Madre, Guatemala's jungles, the mountains of Nepal, India's Ladakh region, Australia, New Zealand, Indonesia, England, Wales, Portugal, Greece, Egypt, Sri Lanka, the Caribbean, Tonga, Western Samoa, the Dominican Republic, and Canada's Arctic region.

I traveled always alone and as simply and economically as I possibly could, with a knapsack, a tent, light cooking gear, cameras and film, and small gifts to give to people who befriended me along the way. Sewing needles, pens and pencils, balloons, and Polaroid pictures were always well received. I often brought photographs of my village in Vermont, as people were often curious to see images of America—the blazing foliage of autumn, the deep drifted snows of winter, family farms, our village church, and snapshots of friends and neighbors.

Each country that I traveled to was alluring and interesting in its own way. The mountains and deserts, the high steppes and tundra, the islands and moors, and the rain forest jungles all awakened in me a deep sense of appreciation and a fuller understanding of my own life. My senses were bathed in the clear blue sea, my mind cleared by the songs of the wind in the trees.

The different cultures proved to be empowering teachers too. Each village, each family, reflected new ways of living. The Nepalese, for example, could grow a year's supply of food on a plot of ground not much bigger than a house. The Inuit, who gave their babies away to those with none, taught me unconditional love. The Native Americans held a reverence for the natural world, Grandfather Sky and Mother Earth. The Maoris knew the joy of singing. The Australian Aborigines believed that the dream world was more real than the ordinary world. The Scots had learned to accept the weather, the Tibetans their fate. The Mexicans loved laughter and practical jokes. The Samoans believed that whoever appeared on their doorstep became family.

Coming to rest in Vermont after nearly twenty years of travel, I desired to share the faces and stories of hundreds of people who had befriended me along the way. Foremost were the strong women and the gentle men. This is a book about gentle men.

Why was I drawn to these men over a twenty-year period? What was the intrigue? One might assume it was because of their rustic lifestyle, which etched their faces with character. And that was true. Some might assume that I was attempting to record remote cultures at the edge of change. And that, too, was correct. But ultimately my reasons were not in the men's appearances, nor in their rural and indigenous cultures. It was in the simplicity and goodness of their lives.

My own spiritual path conspired to lead me to these men. I sensed my karma ripening each time I stood before them. As one feels humbled and inspired simply by being in the same room with a holy person, I felt exhilarated and softened as I came to know these men. Attending a cowboy birthing calves on the prairie, sitting with sixty Tongan men as they sang

devotional songs for the earth and the sky and the water, fishing with Gaelic men on the banks of the Outer Hebrides—these, and a thousand more, brought me great joy and inspiration.

I met hundreds—thousands—of wonderful men. I could speak of many with fantastic tales. One, however, stands out as extraordinary. He was, I believe, the most beautifully spirited and gentle man I ever knew. His name was Harry Smith, and he was an old hired man on a farm in Vermont. He was close to sixty when I met him. For twenty-five years he and I shared a boundless relationship. I set up my tepee in his north pasture and shared life with him. Harry became the grandfather I never had.

The first time I ever met Harry Smith he was standing in the manger of a barn prying out his tooth with a claw hammer. He was a rugged individualist who did not put much stock in modern conveniences like dentists, hospitals, doctors, and bills that put you into debt. So Harry often did things his own way. In fact, Harry was the most independent, old-fashioned, and originally pure-minded man I ever knew.

Most notables are often described by the things they accomplished or the things they owned in their short span of years. But with Harry, I often describe him in relation to all the things he did not do, or did not own, or did not pretend to be. I once made a list of over one hundred things he had never done. This, to me, was a direct correlation to the character of the man. The list's beginning went something like this: never slept out of his own bed; never left the state of Vermont; never wore shorts; never wore a tie; never went to a doctor, dentist, lawyer, banker; never drove a car; never rode in a train, plane, boat, or bus; never went into debt; never had electricity; never owned a telephone or a television; never had running water or indoor plumbing; never stole, or lied, or cheated; never had an enemy.

Stepping onto Harry's old sagging porch amid the clutter of a hundred jumbled pieces of free things he had found along the roadsides, I felt the real world ceased to exist. A visit could last up to six hours. "What's your rush?" he would ask. "We've got all the time in the world." And a fifth cat would jump onto his

lap, and the day seemed to melt and become sweeter.

The enjoyment of visiting with Harry was not in the fact that he and everything around him looked like remnants from the nineteenth century. Nor was it in the eccentricities of the man's life: the three pairs of overalls he often wore to keep warm, the thirteen calendars on the soiled walls of his kitchen, the nine ticking pocket watches on the walls that each kept a different time. It was, first and foremost, Harry's mind and Harry's heart and Harry's gentleness. He was his own person, nearly untouched by modern times, a vestigial remain of a bygone era. As a near hermit, he carried in his being the quietude of a gentler time. His own peace and inner wisdom were the blessings bestowed upon friends.

As a gentle man, Harry Smith was a very popular man. Women especially felt an attraction to the man, even though initially they might express a touch of self-consciousness being with such an old-fashioned farmhand. Though a dyed-in-the-wool bachelor, Harry was ever gracious and outgoing while visiting with women. Several women told me that he was the most genteel man they had ever met. They emphasized that he made them feel "lovely and pure." It was his courtesies—the way he doffed his cap, or politely sat listening, or how he walked beside a friend.

Such was the heart of Harry Smith. And such were the hearts and minds of hundreds of other men leading quiet lives in small villages around the world. The planet so desperately needs more of their kind. With violence and chaos rampant, men worldwide need to step forward individually and affirm gentleness as a way of life.

Compassion for all living things is the highest tenet of all religions, all realizations. It comes about to all those who seek it with an open heart. As surely as the sun appears each morning, gentleness and compassion for all living things—enemies and adversaries included—can rise like sweetgrass smoke to the four quarters of the universe. It is as simple as breathing in and out a natural respect for all life.

The men's lives portrayed here in photograph and story stand as a quiet record to loving kindness and gentleness. May these good and kindly faces continue to inspire others as they did me. May all beings come to their own awakening. May all beings be happy. And may our beautiful planet—our home—resonate with peace and understanding till the end of time.

Ethan Hubbard
Chelsea, Vermont

THE FACE OF A MAN

It was easy to meet the Maori people. Tourists were few and far between. John, a traditional Maori who wore the facial tatoo of his ancestors, found me wandering in the hills behind his village one afternoon. It was his custom to walk for hours in the forest each day. He insisted I come back to his little cabin, a bachelor's nest that was spare and rustic, where he made a delicious tea from herbs gathered in the hills. He sweetened it with honey from his hives.

Tsetan and I worked beside the villagers in the fields, harvesting barley. I found joy in this work: in the golden grain that shone in the sun, in the singing that rose from all corners of the field. The men chanted one long chorus, and the women and children sang a sweet refrain. These were songs, chants, and rounds centuries old. Often I was asked to hold a two-year-old boy while his parents worked nearby. The little one came easily into my arms, and I would hold him close as I walked the fields. Language between us didn't seem to matter—a tickle in his small ribs brought forth peals of laughter from both of us.

FATHER AND SON
NEAR LEH, LADAKH, INDIA

FATHER AND SON
OLLANTAYTAMBO, PERU

The walls of the granite mountains were bathed in dreamy winter's light, pale yellow and wan upon the dry stalks of corn and the eucalyptus leaves that lay like a carpet on the trail. *Campesinos* came down from the mountain fields with their small bands of cattle, sheep, and goats, and old Indian teamsters with long wooden plows resting upon their broad shoulders drove oxen and steers before them. Woodcutters in ragged homespun leggings descended the trail with their burros and small horses ladened with split green wood.

I lived by the Sonora River for more than a week, camping beside it, walking its banks every day, and visiting with the local families who worked small *milpas* (farms) growing corn and beans. They were friendly country people. Most of them had never seen a *norteamericano* before, let alone spoken to one. I saw them down by the river in the cotton-wood trees with their sheep and cattle, whispering in small groups as they watched me. I tried to keep a pot of coffee on my campfire during the day, and when I beckoned to them, they came up in groups of two and three and sat on the earth by the fire. We spoke in Spanish, drank cups of strong coffee, and ate handfuls of trail mix from a wooden bowl. They were good honest people who liked to joke and laugh. A frequent visitor to my campsite was a one-legged nut gatherer by the name of Socorro Gonzales. Two or three times a week he would pass my camp on his burro with sacks of shelled pecans hanging from the saddle. Agile as a schoolboy, he would climb upon his burro and then hoist himself into the limbs of the trees to gather the nuts.

I always took the west way to the plaza in the morning for my strong Greek coffee at Adonio's Cafenio. Maybe it was because the sunshine fell on those hilly side streets more generously during these chilly December mornings. Quite often I would encounter the smell of frankincense in the air, a smell like no other in the world, and a few streets beyond I would see the tall bearded Greek priest carrying a tin saucer with the "smudge pot" of burning frankincense.

Mustafa made tea for me again this chilly winter morning. I loved watching him build the small fire of twigs that he judiciously laid between small white rocks, blowing upon the flames with great billowing cheeks. When the water was hot, he would walk off to a garden and return with fresh mint. The tea was delicious sweetened with honey. Everyone said that Mustafa made the best tea in the oasis and that it tasted different from women's tea—that it had his energy.

The men in Sri Lanka tried to teach me to enjoy chewing the arica they so dearly loved. In a wooden pestle they ground up the nuts, adding a dollop of lime, a touch of local tobacco, and wrapped the concoction in a green leaf. Most of the time I swallowed a bit of the tart mixture and nearly choked to death, much to the gentle, discreet laughter of the hopeful old men. But I never gave up trying.

GREEK ORTHODOX PRIEST

AYASSOS, LÉSVOS, GREECE

MUSTAFA

FARAFRA OASIS, EGYPT

FARMER, GRINDING TOBACCO

SRI LANKA

HASSAN SHABEN, FARMER
FARAFRA OASIS, EGYPT

JOHN MACLEAN, CROFTER
OUTER HEBRIDES, SCOTLAND

LOUIS PAGA, ABORIGINE
ALICE SPRINGS, AUSTRALIA

I came upon twelve old men playing a game called *Ellap Siga* in the sand. My friend Hassan told me that it was as old as the Great Pyramid. Twenty-five walnut-sized stones, half black and half white, were scrupulously arranged in quadrants like army phalanxes. The men would shout out expletives as they snatched an opponent's rock in a sly move. Just desert stones in the sand and gnarled old hands and sly eyes—where invisible thoughts could steal an opponent's stone in a flash.

"That's right, laddie. Keep the center of the stack of the haycock higher than the edges, that's the trick. And be sure to stack the bundles clockwise, as that's the direction that the sun travels. We islanders have tried to stay in tune with nature as best we can for all these years."

The Aborigines were dying a slow, horrifying death. Their nomadic ways, their art, dance, music, and oral history, which stretched back to the last Ice Age—all they possessed—had slipped through their hands like sand. They endured this collective suffering with quiet resignation. Perhaps their acceptance stemmed from their belief that this life was a mere shadow of the real world, that beyond it lay a greater reality.

SIPRIEN FUTURI, QUECHUA

OLLANTAYTAMBO, PERU

Hiking along the Patacancha River, I met an exceptional 90-year-old man driving

gaunt goats before him with a switch. His old and twisted mouth voiced Quechua words I could not

comprehend and in his face I beheld an Inca.

OLD DESCHINI, NAVAJO MEDICINE MAN
MANY FARMS, ARIZONA, UNITED STATES

I made supper for Old Deschini as promised at Fred and Mary Tayah's house above Canyon de Chelly.

The old man took off his hat and coat, talked with Fred in Navajo for a few minutes,

and then sat down at the table and waited for his meal in silence. When it arrived, he seized the plate with both

hands and drew it close to him with his long, slender fingers. No talk, no eye contact.

When he had finished, he pushed his plate away and looked up slowly, smiling in appreciation.

The men of the oasis enjoyed sitting in the winter sunshine in their *galebeas*. At the first rays of the sun coming over the desert from the east, one man at a time emerged from their earthen homes to crouch up against the walls, like pigeons, to be joined by others. In the afternoon when the sands were warm they broke up into smaller groups. One man spun wool every day. He seemed to pray at the same time and the skeins of gathered yarn reminded me of prayer beads.

I gave a lift to a Taos Pueblo elder
who was hitchhiking home from
Wal-Mart to his ancient pueblo.
Along the way we took time to sit
together under giant cottonwood
trees to watch a rainbow that hung
majestically over the Sangre de
Cristo Mountains.

How beautiful to see a man fall
to his knees and pray. The Gujar
shepherd carefully placed his prayer
rug upon the stony ground,
turned westward toward Mecca,
and unabashedly prostrated his
body, touching the earth with his
forehead.

One afternoon Old Deschini took
me down into Canyon de Chelly on
a steep treacherous trail where
cedars spanned great chasms and
where fingerholds in the cliffs were
no bigger than buttons.

TAOS PUEBLO ELDER
TAOS, NEW MEXICO, UNITED STATES

GUJAR SHEPHERD
KASHMIR, INDIA

OLD DESCHINI, NAVAJO MEDICINE MAN
MANY FARMS, ARIZONA, UNITED STATES

Union Island had a magic that pervaded the earth, and water, and sky, and the two thousand people who called the tiny island home. On my last day I trudged up Good for Nothing Hill and said morning prayers. Then I ran barefoot down to Ashton Village where I found my friend Mr. Stewart eating mangoes under a tree with young Willicia.

Morning came early to the high Andes. Sunshine slid sideways into my tent and by seven the Quechua Indians were already working in the fields. I looked toward the mountains and could spot nearly thirty columns of blue smoke rising into the air from small homes high above me on the slopes. My friend Domingo came into view. He was milking his cow by the stream. Spontaneously I grabbed a bag of coffee and yelled to him and little Benigno in Spanish: "You bring the milk; I'll bring the coffee. We'll make cafe con leche."

My son Taylor and I came to a gathering of tents and tepees in the Umpqua National Forest at close to 7,000 feet elevation. As the rains cleared and a new crescent moon peeked out through the mists that draped this high clearing, five thousand of us stood patiently talking in whispers as we waited for our dinner to be served from a communal kitchen of boiling cauldrons in the forest. We stood in concentric circles in the ensuing dusk, wooden bowls in our hands, caked mud on our bare feet. Someone in our midst began an incantation of "om" and five thousand voices joined in. The valley was ringed with light.

WILLIAM STEWART AND WILLICIA

UNION ISLAND, ST. VINCENT AND THE GRENADINES

DOMINGO AND BENIGNO, QUECHUA

HUILLOC, PERU

RAINBOW FAMILY GATHERING

UMPQUA NATIONAL FOREST, OREGON, UNITED STATES

I remembered when I last stopped here. It must have been in 1979 when Phil Connaughton was 79. I recalled how he would open his shop precisely at nine o'clock, feed his thirteen cats, and put his feet up on his rolltop desk and wait for customers. Eleven years later I figured he would be dead. But not so. When I pulled into the old tire shop I was amazed to find Phil there. He remembered me and we laughed some about the years gone by. At 90 Phil still opened his shop precisely at nine, fed his thirteen cats, and put his feet up on the rolltop desk. The difference now was that he had nothing to sell. He just pretended to be in business.

As a fine captain and a gifted navigator, Festus Hutchinson had spent most of his life on tankers around the world. Now in his retirement he had built his own cargo boat and ferried passengers and gear between the islands. He was a tall, strong man with luminous blue-green eyes, the color of the Caribbean waters.

A cool calm ran through the man. I could feel it when I shook hands with him, and saw it as he coursed the challenging waters off Carriacou Island in a storm. I would have followed him anywhere.

WILLIE MacPHERSON AND IAN PAUL

OUTER HEBRIDES, SCOTLAND

He placed his arm around the boy's shoulder, showing him the various components of the engine. They were a handsome sight standing there, with sea birds circling overhead and the water shimmering like a million diamonds.

After a lunch of sandwiches and hot coffee, we rested. As the boat rolled gently on the giant swells that lumbered in off the Atlantic's vast expanse, Willie stood with young Ian Paul in the stern.

OLD NINO, MAORI

MATAHI, NEW ZEALAND

HERMAN BARR

AT HIS BIRTHPLACE, NORTH DAKOTA, UNITED STATES

The grandfather, a leathery-faced Maori with a long white beard and woolly head of hair, waited for my return. His name was Nino Tacao, and he lived in a small cabin by the creek. He plowed his garden with an old white horse and put up fruits and vegetables for the winter. He hunted on the mountain slopes nearby, following trails that had been made by his people a thousand years ago. Deer, possum, wild pigs and goats, game birds, and rodents were his staples. Green eels, however, were his delicacy, and on moonlit nights when the mist floated above the stream, Nino took me by torchlight to wander barefoot in pools where we netted the five-foot-long slimy creatures.

Mr. Barr took me and my 11-year-old son Taylor out on the prairies and showed me the hole in the

ground where he was born. He explained: "My dad didn't have a sod house. To have a soddy you needed to

have a plow and a yoke of oxen or a team of horses to pull the plow. My mom and dad had neither,

only a pick and a shovel and strong backs. So they shoveled out a dugout in the side of a hill, and we lived

there from 1885 to 1895."

Two long weeks trekking on the winding mountain trails brought us to the fringe of the high Tibetan Plateau and

our first Buddhist village, Pisang. There we stayed with a Tibetan family. Their rude house had a single smoky room

illuminated by candles and several fireplaces. An old father and grandfather sat cross-legged on the hearth spin-

ning prayer wheels in one hand and counting wooden prayer beads in the other. Above them on the mantel was

the family altar with burning candles, a wooden Buddha, and a picture of the Dalai Lama.

BAPTISM

SAN JOSÉ, PETÉN, GUATEMALA

"SCRUFFY"

AT THE HOT SPRING NEAR TAOS, NEW MEXICO

UNITED STATES

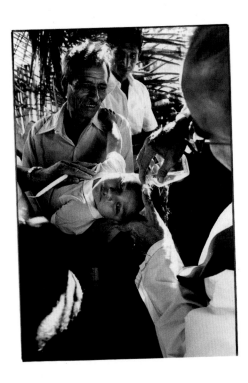

These were the descendants of the great pyramid builders of
Mesoamerica. They grew crops of corn and beans and fished
in the blue-green waters from dugout canoes. Most of the villagers still spoke Mayan, and a few still worshiped Mayan
gods. The marriage of two religions came alive when I saw an
Indian boy being baptized in a tiny church made of palm
fronds.

Scruffy worked hard with a newspaper delivery

service in the big city. At day's end when he

pulled into Taos and his home, he was ready to

unwind in a hot spring down along the Rio

Grande. He said that when the sunset bled crim-

son on the beautiful Sangre de Cristo Mountains,

his anointment was complete.

I met Daniel Womack, a blind gospel jubilee singer, at a concert in a church. Afterward, as we spoke in the shade of a giant sycamore tree, I asked him about himself. "I have a mission in life just the same as my parents. I sing the praises of the Lord in song for all the world to hear. There is no greater gift I can give to this world."

Art Storley, a retired railroad worker, lived in his old house out on the prairie. After visiting with him, I realized he had two daily practices that I envied: he read the local newspaper cover to cover every afternoon on his porch, and he played a few tunes on his violin, whether anyone was listening or not.

I tiptoed to the doorway of the children's room where John was softly playing lullabies on his banjo to Molly, Edith, and Elsie as they drifted off to sleep. John once told me that in twelve years he had only missed a couple of times in their nightly lullaby ritual.

DANIEL WOMACK, BLIND GOSPEL SINGER

ROANOKE, VIRGINIA, UNITED STATES

ART STORLEY, RETIRED RAILROAD WORKER

AMBROSE, NORTH DAKOTA, UNITED STATES

JOHN GAWLER, FATHER OF THREE

BELGRADE LAKES, MAINE, UNITED STATES

At sunset Taulelei would take his new grandson in his arms and carry him about the yard showing him the immediate world. "This is a pig, and this is a chicken. Here is fire, and here is a coconut tree."

Before returning to the house the grandfather often held the baby up to the sky, offering him back to the universe itself.

Gabriel sat in a rickety chair at the door's entrance and inscribed Dora's name, age, and date in the family Bible. This was the one-hundredth genera-tion on the land. Despite all—the revolution, the road that never came, the absence of doctors and nurses, the broken sandals and the mud-caked door-way—another Quechua speaker, a daughter called Dora, had come to live and farm in these high Andes.

TAULELEI AND GRANDSON TOESE
SAFUA, SAVAI'I, WESTERN SAMOA

GABRIEL, RECORDING THE BIRTH OF HIS DAUGHTER
OLLANTAYTAMBO, PERU

DONALD MacCORMICK, CROFTER
OUTER HEBRIDES, SCOTLAND

Sundays were special times with the MacCormicks. We went to church as a family. After the breakfast dishes had been done and the geese and chickens fed, the older sisters heated up huge pans of water on the stove for Donald, Angus, and me to shave with. They pressed our pants and white shirts with an old iron heated on the peat stove, and then they made us march around in a circle as they inspected their handiwork. Kate Effie sometimes took me by the hand and made me pirouette, like some circus dancer—"Ah, handsome as a prince, not like some waif who lives in the hayloft."

I saw old Fred Metcalf on his great-grandfather's farm along the Connecticut River. He was about to steal away from his barn chores (again) to catch an organ recital across the river at Dartmouth College. He told me he always wanted to be a classical musician, but he had to keep cows all of his life to stay alive. With a great sigh he told me that he would have traded in all the cows just to have heard Bach play the organ once.

The man at the general store told me that a hermit lived in a deep forest out of town and that he occasionally saw

visitors. I went and was greeted by a polite little man of 70 who chose to live a simple life. Chop wood, carry water,

and look for good in everything. That was his philosophy.

PERCY TOHLOPH, FARMER

AHUROA, NEW ZEALAND

OLD TOMBA

NEAR MARFA, NEPAL

The commune people loved Percy Tohloph. He could always be counted on to dig a ditch for them with his backhoe or deliver manure for their fruit trees. The young people on the commune reciprocated by cooking the old bachelor a special dinner of roast chicken and gravy and garden vegetables with a blackberry pie and fresh whipped cream for dessert. Percy would linger after the meal with his coffee and a smoke. In the lamplight, with a child or two on his lap, he sat and talked for hours. When he was leaving, someone inevitably put a loaf of freshly baked bread under his arm.

Kipa and I stayed with an old hermit named Tomba who lived alone with his cat. We enjoyed Tomba immensely. There was an intrinsic joy in the old man's monastic way of life. I envied him; he seemed happy with so very little. Sometimes we would work beside him in his garden pulling weeds. And once we climbed to the top of his sagging roof and repaired the holes with new bamboo and thatch. At night we slept beside each other on the earthen hearth as the dying coals pulsed in the grate and two crickets sang closeby.

Across the main road from my guesthouse was a district of the Ambepussa village called Danowita. It was a poorer area than the area encompassed by the broad valley of rice paddies. The people of Danowita worked mud and straw into bricks for the village houses. They were especially fond of having me photograph them, and whenever they saw me coming along the worn pathways of the jungle they lined up with hopeful expressions on their faces.

I watched the movie *Dances with Wolves* with a Navajo family on their reservation at Cow Creek. My VW bus sat outside beneath the juniper trees. I was merely spending the night, and in the morning would move on. Jimmie, who had brought me to meet his family, took me across the mesa to a cabin at the base of the mountains. There I was introduced to his 85-year-old grandfather, Kenneth Begay. The old man, who could speak no English, had no electricity to watch television movies and expressed sadness that he could offer me nothing. He motioned, however, for me to sit beside him as he gestured to the golden light on the mountains.

KENNETH BEGAY, NAVAJO SHEPHERD

COW CREEK, ARIZONA, UNITED STATES

OMAR GABRIL, SUFI ELDER

FARAFRA OASIS, EGYPT

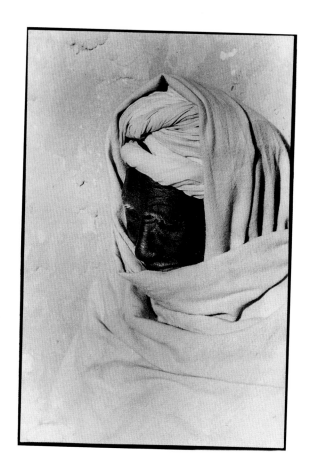

The zikr (remembrance) was held on Sunday evening at the old Sufi's home near the date grove.
Ten men sat on the floor in a dimly lit room. Omar Gabril read directly from the
Sufi text and the evening proceeded like a scripture study. The night was filled with whispers and chants
while a cold desert wind moaned about the eaves.

I met an old hermit by the name of Otis Beech. He lived in a caved-in cabin beside a roaring stream in a hollow south of the Blue Ridge Mountains. He kept bees and often used the fine comb honey to barter produce in Hayesville. There was something deeply refreshing in the man. I think it had something to do with his owning nearly nothing.

I picked up a foot traveler crossing through the Ruby Mountains near Elko. I asked him where he was from and where he might be headed. "Nowhere in particular." Then he explained. "A tramp like myself isn't like a homeless person or a hitchhiker. They're heading somewhere fast. Tramps on the other hand aren't heading anywhere special. We're enjoying right where we are already."

OTIS BEECH WITH COMB HONEY
HAYESVILLE, NORTH CAROLINA
UNITED STATES

WALLY FAYANT, CREE
TRAMPING ACROSS NEVADA
UNITED STATES

Old Deschini was fascinating to be around: tall, silent, and mystical. He had the most amazing eyes I had ever seen, luminous pools of turquoise, and his hands were large and smooth as a snake's skin.

He did not speak English and I did not speak Navajo, but we got on well together. He sensed I wished to learn about the desert, the canyon, and the history of his people.

In late October we had a full day of lobstering on the Atlantic. From dawn to dusk we skirted the banks of the Hebrides in an old wooden boat called the *Golden August,* throwing out and hauling in close to seventy wooden creels. Enormous quantities of rope and lines and floats were dispensed without a single tangle or knot.

PETER HAGGERTY, MERCHANT MARINE

OUTER HEBRIDES, SCOTLAND

WILLIE MACPHERSON, FISHERMAN

OUTER HEBRIDES, SCOTLAND

Tsetan and I traveled like desert nomads, putting in long hard days between villages. We traveled through high valleys strewn with boulders where eagles and vultures soared in the dull wintry skies. Jagged peaks rose into the snow clouds. For several days we climbed up a mountain trail without seeing anyone, sleeping at night by a small fire we made with dried yak dung. There was a harsh beauty to this part of the trek: in the biting wind that tore at our faces, in the courage and stamina of our little horses, and in our silence as we lay in our blankets at night.

Dawn broke clear and windless and first light streaked the flanks of Nilgiri with pinks and violets. Down below

my tent the village came to life. Roosters crowed, women took goats to the hills, children washed and readied for

school. On a stone terrace a young man in black meditated at the brink of the great canyon.

At his prompting I removed my clothes and put them in a pile at the base of a juniper tree. The old man walked around in a circle for a minute or two—like an old brown lizard about to burrow in the sand—and then pointed to a spot where he instructed me to lie down. Then he left me, walking down the canyon the way we had come. I scooped up handfuls of the hot sand and covered my entire body, leaving only my head free. Something in me let go, and I felt as if I was melting down into the warm earth. I drifted in and out of consciousness and listened to the trickle of the stream a few yards away and to the sound of a warbler in the bush. When I awoke, perhaps an hour later, the stiffness and weariness had disappeared from my body, and I lay up against the base of a tree watching white clouds in the sky forming and reforming in the early evening.

Roland Choquette and Glen Duger

Woodbury, Vermont, United States

I stopped in to see Glen Duger on his ninetieth birthday and found Roland Choquette also at the cabin. In good humor, they were drinking a six-pack of beer and swapping cattle-dealing stories. Old Glen outdid himself by telling how he froze the toes off his right foot three years back when he returned a bit tipsy to his cabin after a dance and fell asleep at thirty below zero with his foot sticking out of the covers.

The Chase Brothers, Scything the Lower Meadow

Middlesex, Vermont, United States

Sharing the noon meal with the Chases was like stepping back through time. Their 81-year-old mother served things mostly from off the farm: roast chicken, dumplings and gravy, Kennebec potatoes, carrots, apple pie, and fresh milk from their cow. They were a resourceful and energetic family, typical of the mountain people who once populated the Appalachians from Maine to Georgia.

Phillip Masey and Gordon Sullivan, Ranch Neighbors

Whitewater, Colorado, United States

I pulled into the dooryard of a ranch for directions and found two men sitting on the porch watching the day go by. They introduced themselves and shared that they had been neighbors for forty years. I asked them to remember a good time they had had together. They told me that once back in the 1920s they had driven an old Model T Ford to the Grand Canyon for a camping trip. Upon retelling the story they laughed heartily.

In a tiny village called Tal, on the far side of the Annapurnas, I spent the night with one of the many *ammas* (mothers) that Kipa, my Sherpa, knew along the way. As I wandered through the village, I met a Tibetan-looking man resting on a stone bench in the late afternoon sunshine. "Are you Tibetan?" I asked him. "No," he replied, "Larki man." He wore his hair in two long braids bound together with strips of red cloth. His cloak and ripped leggings smelled of damp wool and rancid grease. On his feet he wore yakskin boots. He eyed my camera on the bench between us, picked it up, and aimed it at the surrounding peaks, muttering faint ahhs and mmms all the while at the way the telephoto lens made distant things look close. The boy, who appeared not to be related to the man, seemed content—like Aladdin—to hold his lamp and giggle at the two of us old men at play with camera and words.

I played soccer with the boys until sunset in Ebenezer field. Goats on the hillsides, teenagers playing cricket, tiny pastel houses, and the green palm fronds blowing in the wind reminded me of long, long ago. When dusk came and the path homeward lay in shadows, I kindly accepted the offer of a man and boy who led me through the cassie thorns and forest thickets to the main road.

BILL SNEDIGAR, BLACKSMITH

STEVENSVILLE, MONTANA, UNITED STATES

HARRY SMITH, FARMHAND

WAITSFIELD, VERMONT, UNITED STATES

I found a great blacksmith who had a sign in his shop that read: "If we can't fix it, don't break it." His name was Bill Snedigar and he was carrying on the blacksmith tradition of his Dutch father and grandfather.

Harry chided me with humor again for calling a hatchet an ax. Before he had caught me calling spikes "nails," and he went into a comical lecture about how an ex-school-teacher like myself was supposed to know the correct names of things. I made a mental note that I had better get used to calling the noon meal dinner and not lunch.

The captain often read to us poems he had written. He read them slowly in a beautiful thick voice, and he paused once in a while to look up at us. The poems were mostly about a man's love for a woman, perhaps about his departed wife.

He poured us glasses of whiskey between readings and grinned at young Ian Paul as they toasted in Gaelic.

ROMEO BEAUDRY

WATCHING WINTER SETTLE IN

NORTHERN VERMONT, UNITED STATES

On cold winter nights I often went to see Romeo at his farm along the Canadian border. He and I would talk of early Vermont, and inevitably Romeo would tell me his feats of wood-chopping.

"Hell, I put up two cords of four-foot-length hardwood with just a double-bitted ax in a single day. Started at dawn and didn't get home till dark."

ARTHUR ROBERTS

LLANFACHRETH, WALES

DAFYD GRIFFITH

LLANFACHRETH, WALES

When I asked the
two old Welsh
shepherds how
long they had been
gathering sheep off
the mountain,
Arthur replied:
"If I had a pound
note for every time
I dragged my
feet across this
mountain on the
sheep gathers,
you'd be looking
at a very rich man.

Dafyd and I went
to kindergarten
together and here
we are at the end
of our lives still
good neighbors
and still helping
each other out."

The gather on the mountain brought down a thousand or more sheep. Arthur, Dafyd, Rhys, and Idris sorted theirs with uncanny precision, thirteen black and white dogs working on the immense mob. The men used the ancient holding pens of stone built by their ancestors. It was a good place to hand-shear too. I watched Lewis Williams from Tyddyn Bach shearing a rogue ewe just as his father and grandfather and great-grandfather had done on the same spot.

Snow began falling at dusk. I watched from a bank of cedars at the marsh's edge. Andrew's girlfriend appeared. The two spoke in sign language, since they both were deaf and mute. Snow drifted in on sheets of winter cold and made the characters surreal, ethereal.

Eleven hundred miles from New Zealand in the middle of nowhere, on a remote island, in a remote island group, is a far-flung Polynesian nation called Tonga. No electricity, no stores, no telephones, no roads, no cars. Walking along jungle paths like a child, listening to men singing in the bush as they work their fields of yams and taro, I thought I had stumbled into another century.

Lewis Williams, Sheep Farmer

Llanfachreth, Wales

Andrew Dana, Passamaquoddy, On the Trap Line

St. Ann Reservation, Maine, United States

Taro Farmer

Fakakakai, Ha'ano, Ha'apai, Tonga

He lived alone in the mountains and made his living by whittling mountain laurel into fanciful necklaces, belts, and rings. Some called him a hermit, but he did not consider himself one. He was gregarious and looked forward to all the visitors he had, especially the high school students in the Foxfire program who trudged up through the hollow to see him. They said that he was "neat." He was quite fascinated by the young "hippies" who showed special interest in his wooden jewelry.

KENNY RUNION

MOUNTAIN CITY, GEORGIA, UNITED STATES

CLAUDIO, QUECHUA

HUILLOC, PERU

Thirty Quechua male dancers in bright red tunics and long white birdlike wings descended the trail with visceral shrieks and unearthly cries. My heart flew up to meet them. When they reached the village where women and children sat, the leader, Claudio, beckoned me to join them in the celebration.

Old Safi hitched his

roan horse in the shafts

and off we went in his

wagon through a

Tongan twilight.

A man on horseback

passed us with six fine

horses on lead ropes.

Greetings were called

out: "Fefe hake *(How*

are you)?" "Sai pe,

mako *(I am fine).*"

OLD SAFI

HA'ANO, HA'APAI, TONGA

I walked four miles at sunset through the desert to be with Sebastian at his cave. He was weaving a blanket on

a backstrap loom when I arrived. The cave was especially beautiful at night, whitewashed walls and sand floor

with marvelous flickering shadows from a pulsating fire of piñon logs. When the time was right I requested a

story. The old man obliged me by telling how as a young mailman and courier he had run a distance of nearly

six hundred miles in the high Sierras in just under nine days.

Antonio and the Children
Moimenta, Portugal

On rainy days when the streets were amuck with rain and mud and the village children had nothing to do, old Antonio would stand with them in the rain. He would listen to their tales of woe, or blow up their deflated soccer ball, or even initiate a game of tag, remembering a time in his life when he was a boy on these rainy streets in the mountains with nothing to do.

Feliciano Candelario, 96
Loma de Cabrera, The Dominican Republic

Here was an old part of the Americas. I was fifteen miles from the Haitian border on cattle trails walking through a golden valley of small farms. Near sunset I came upon a very old man called Cande sitting with his young granddaughter in a rocking chair. When I asked him what they were doing, he told me that they had been listening to the wind and the birds in the trees.

Harry Smith, Farmhand
Waitsfield, Vermont, United States

I watched old Harry showing young Daniel Von Trapp his 1924 high school picture. "Yup, that's me in the third row. You wouldn't think I was ever that young, would you? That was my junior year. I never went back to finish it out. The principal made a rule the following year that all boys had to wear neckties to school. Hell, you wouldn't catch me in one of them nooses. Anyway, I'd rather have been with the cows."

Old Niu and Grandson
Fakakakai, Ha'ano, Ha'apai, Tonga

Old Niu's legs and hips hurt him and he walked with a labored gait. Still he went to his gardens in the jungle each day with his tools to care for his small plots of taro and yams. I think he did it for the boy. I would watch from afar as the old man pointed out trees and plants and carefully explained things to the boy that would carry him through life.

ALFONSO TESECUN, MAYA

SAN JOSÉ, PETÉN, GUATEMALA

Alfonso took me across the lake

in his dugout canoe to the

family milpa *(farm). A*

traditional Mayan, he planted

by the moon, poured blood over

the new seed corn to insure

fertility, and cleared the land

with ancient tools.

WILLIE MACPHERSON
OUTER HEBRIDES, SCOTLAND

Willie MacPherson was a rugged and handsome-featured fisherman who lived alone in his father's cottage on the peninsula at Uskavagh. Willie was nearing 60, but his strong, muscular body still sashayed as he walked. He said it was from years at sea and from long walks he took crossing the trackless moors in all kinds of weather.

Tongan Farmer with Wife

Fakakakai, Ha'ano, Ha'apai, Tonga

106-year-old Farmer

Farafra Oasis, Egypt

Quechua Farmers

Ollantaytambo, Peru

I watched along with the Tongan farmer's wife as he inched his way up the tall coconut palm tree with bare feet clinging to the coarse trunk. About his head he wore a wreath of braided palm leaves like an emperor's laurel of victory.

At sunset I walked with Mohammed, my teacher friend, out to a small village called Goshna. We came upon a man and two boys in striped tunics loading rich spinach into two lovely baskets on a white donkey. When we asked the man's age, he smiled and said he was 106. He then spryly mounted the donkey side-saddle in one easy vault and rode home for his dinner.

Everyone in Ollantaytambo was a farmer, if not by profession, then by the sheer number of hours spent toiling in the fields. Whether one was a seamstress or a butcher or a baker, one still was a farmer and always connected with the family lands. Early Spanish chroniclers wrote that the Incas intuitively combined relaxation and labor in one breath, not separating work from worship.

The monastery below the temples was the home of seven monks, young men in their late teens and early twenties. The grounds surrounding the monastery were filled with spacious gardens and tree-lined lawns. I loved watching the shadows fall about the monastery in the late afternoon and the orange-robed monks walking with each other as they inspected young fruit trees or flower beds. We saw each other from time to time. Our communion was always simple and direct: a smile, a slight bow, sometimes a flower given.

SADHU ON PILGRIMAGE

NEAR LUMLE, NEPAL

He told me in broken English that prior to becoming a Hindu sadhu, a spiritual mendicant, he had been a banker, head of his family, and a householder complete with an automobile. But then in midlife he felt an urging to become more spiritual and follow asceticism, to renounce the ordinary life.

In a village called Birethante, my Sherpa guide Kipa and I entered a smoky room filled with people and ani-

mals, a loft somewhat between a stable and a house. The porters sat in a circle eating and drinking. They

made room for us and passed food and drink our way—strong beer and a plate of coagulated sheep's blood and

goats' feet. For a split second I hesitated, but then I said a prayer and began to eat. It tasted very good. The

beer and goats' feet kept coming all night long, as did the wild music of drums and flutes and dancing.

I lay sleeping in a wooden ox cart in the autumn sunshine as my host gathered chestnuts in a grove nearby. I awoke to a man on his white burro peering down into the cart as if I might be cargo to carry to market. The burro sniffed me and snorted, and the old man, unaccustomed to seeing strangers in his town, called for others to come examine me.

Fa'a Samoa was a code of life for the Samoan
people. It meant being good to all aspects of life.
To insure that this code continued down through
the ages, village councils met regularly in circles to
discuss everything about village life: whose pigs
had trampled gardens, what teenager was drinking, how foul language had invaded the schools.
Similarly, the churches held regular meetings
where the deacons discussed the spiritual side of
daily life.

Ambepussa had a small store in the jungle. Local
produce was unloaded from oxcarts that came up
from Warkopola. Every day the old men of the village gathered at the store. There were usually
eight or ten regulars, bare-chested and dressed in
colorful sarongs with their white hair tied back in
small neat buns. Whenever I came, one of the old
men inevitably climbed a tall coconut tree and
brought down a fresh coconut for me to drink from.

When the light off the sea had become flat and made the faces of Peter and Ian Paul seem lined and carved, we made port at Stinky Bay. The day had been memorable, but not profitable— only four lobsters from all the traps. Peter, in true Hebridean fashion, handed me the largest lobster as a gift. "Take it, son. You'll enjoy it." Then he turned and made his way through the dusk toward a small fishing cottage at the water's edge.

Maven Bagley and neighbor Melvin Bell butchered a large ewe after church one Sunday. They said it would go for table meat for the winter for both families. They cooperated this way every autumn. When the job was done we went in for the dinner that Yvonne, Maven's wife, had prepared. It felt good to stand in line with the men at the sink to wash up. I lingered with the hot soapy water on my cold, bloodied hands. Maven waited and held the towel for me.

My Tibetan guide
and I spent a
week in a village
called Marka, a
thousand-year-
old Buddhist
citadel perched
on a cliff over-
looking a small
valley of barley
and wheat fields.

There were wonderful sounds at twilight in the sultry Bali air. Somewhere far below in the deep forest a farmer was taking sap from trees to make into wine. I listened— and heard the whole world encapsulated in the sound of his wooden mallet hitting against the trees. *Thock, thock, thock.*

Arthur told me a joke as we waited for the other shepherds. "Why is it a good time to date a lassie when the heather is in bloom? . . . Because the heather is always in bloom."